FAST FACTS
Amazing Universe

KINGFISHER
NEW YORK

KINGFISHER
LONDON & NEW YORK

Copyright © Macmillan Publishers International Ltd 2016
Published in the United States by Kingfisher,
175 Fifth Ave., New York, NY 10010
Kingfisher is an imprint of Macmillan Children's Books, London
All rights reserved.

Distributed in the U.S. and Canada by Macmillan,
175 Fifth Ave., New York, NY 10010

Library of Congress Cataloging-in-Publication data
has been applied for.

Interior design by Tall Tree Ltd
Cover design by Peter Clayman

Adapted from an original text by Philip Steele
Literacy consultants: Kerenza Ghosh, Stephanie Laird

ISBN 978-0-7534-7276-7 (HB)
ISBN 978-0-7534-7277-4 (PB)

Kingfisher books are available for special promotions
and premiums. For details contact: Special Markets
Department, Macmillan, 175 Fifth Ave.,
New York, NY 10010.

For more information, please visit
www.kingfisherbooks.com

Printed in China
9 8 7 6 5 4 3 2
2TR/1016/WKT/UG/128MA

Picture credits
The Publisher would like to thank the following for permission to reproduce their material.
Top = t; Bottom = b; Center = c; Left = l; Right = r
Front cover iStock/snezhanna; Back cover NASA; Pages 1 NASA; 3 NASA; 6br Science Photo Library (SPL)/Jerry Lodriguss; 7bl SPL/David A. Hardy, Futures: 50 Yrs in Space; 9br SPL/Allan Morton/Dennis Milon; 8l SPL/ International Astronomical Union/Martin Kornmesser; 8cl SPL/UK Geological Survey; 8c SPL/NASA; 9tr SPL/ Claus Lunau/FOCI/Bonnier Publications; 9bl SPL/Detlev van Ravenswaay; 9c SPL/Mark Garlick; 9br SPL/ Friedrich Saurer; 10b Arcticphoto/Argnar Sigurdsson; 10–11SPL/Mehau Kulkyk; 11tl Tim Van Sant, ST9 Solar Sail Team Lead, NASA Goddard Space Flight Center; 11c SPL/Scharmer et al, Royal Swedish Academy of Sciences: 11cb Corbis/Roger Ressmeyer: 11r SPL; 12t ESA/NASA; 12c SPL/US Geological Survey; 13tr SPL/ NASA; 14tr SPL/Bernard Edmaier; 14c SPL/Colin Cuthbert; 15tl Corbis/Keren Su; 15c PA/AP; 15c and 15cr Corbis/Randy Wells; 15bl Alamy/Steve Bloom Images; 17tr SPL/NASA; 18tl Corbis/NASA/epa; 18cl Corbis/Reuters/NASA; 18cr SPL/NASA; 19tr Corbis/Guido Cozzi; 20cl SPL Mark Garlick; 21b SPL/Detlev van Ravenswaay; 26bl SPL/J-C Cuillandre/Canada-France-Hawaii Telescope; 24cr SPL/NASA/ESA/R. Sahai & J. Trauger, JPL; 25tr SPL/Russell Kightley; 25b SPL Konstantinos Kifondis; 26c SPL/Victor Habbick Visions; 28tr SPL/Julian Baum.

Contents

In the beginning

The **Universe** began 13.7 billion years ago in an immense burst of energy called the Big Bang. The new Universe expanded very rapidly and then began to cool.

Tiny **particles** of **matter** and antimatter formed. Most of these particles destroyed each other in less than one second.

The matter that remained was not spread evenly. **Gravity** in dense areas of matter (the blue areas below) attracted even more matter.

The cause of the Big Bang is the greatest mystery of science.

The rate of expansion suddenly increased.

Zero time

Less than one-trillionth of a second

One second

100,000 years

TOP FIVE BITESIZE FACTS

 Before the Big Bang there was no space, no matter, and no time. There was nothing.

 By observing light from very far away, we can see stars as they looked billions of years ago.

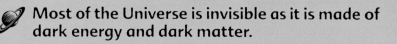 The Sun is about 9 billion years younger than the age of the Universe.

 Most of the Universe is invisible as it is made of dark energy and dark matter.

The temperature in outer space today is −455 °F (−270 °C). That's about three times colder than Antarctica.

The early Universe changed very rapidly, and then the pace of change slowed, so this timeline of key events is not to scale.

antimatter
Material made of antiparticles that cancel out particles.

The Universe cooled to about 5430 °F (3000 °C) and **atoms** (mostly hydrogen) formed from smaller particles.

The first stars formed from hydrogen and helium. These stars produced other new **elements**. When a star died, it exploded as a supernova and scattered the new elements throughout space.

Elements from the first stars helped form the Sun and the other stars that exist today. The temperature has cooled and the rate of expansion has slowed.

380,000
years

560 million
years

13.7 billion
years (today)

Big Chill or Big Rip?

There are two main theories about the future of the Universe. It may continue to expand. The stars would eventually burn out, making everything dark and cold—a Big Chill.

On the other hand, the rate of expansion may increase. **Galaxies**, stars, **planets**, and atoms could tear themselves apart—a Big Rip.

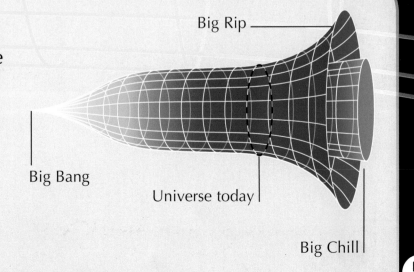

Big Rip

Big Bang

Universe today

Big Chill

Star galaxies

Stars are not evenly spread throughout the Universe. They are grouped into galaxies that may contain millions, billions, or even trillions of stars. Some galaxies are like gigantic whirlpools of stars, while others are more like softly glowing clouds of light.

A dwarf galaxy

No one knows exactly how galaxies form, but they may begin life like this young galaxy. It is a dwarf galaxy, much smaller than our own. The red glow in the center is the light of ancient stars.

New stars burn blue in the outer regions of this young galaxy.

Andromeda

The Andromeda Galaxy is the nearest to our own galaxy, the Milky Way. It is a trillion times brighter than the Sun. It is so far away (2.5 million light-years) that it can be seen only on the darkest nights.

The Whirlpool Galaxy

In spiral galaxies like this (below), the curving arms are marked by lanes of thick, black dust. These are regions where new stars are being born. Like most galaxies, the Whirlpool Galaxy is moving away from us as the Universe expands. Every second, the galaxy moves 300 miles (500 kilometers) farther away.

This fuzzy glow is a small galaxy passing close to the Whirlpool Galaxy. Its gravity may be causing stars to form in the Whirlpool's arms.

TOP FIVE BITESIZE FACTS

🪐 The Milky Way contains an estimated 400 billion stars.

🪐 The Milky Way appears brighter in the hemisphere because the South Pole poi toward the bright galactic core.

🪐 A light-year is the distance traveled by one year.

🪐 Light travels at a speed of 186,000 mile (299,793 kilometers) per second.

🪐 The farthest known galaxy is called EGS and it is 13.2 billion light-years away fro

Our Sun and the Solar System lie in one of the outer arms of the Milky Way.

The Milky Way

The whitish stripe of light in our night sky is our galaxy, the Milky Way. There are billions of stars in our galaxy. Some may have planets in **orbit** around them that are similar to the planets in our Solar System. Our Solar System orbits our local star, the Sun.

Our Solar System

Our Sun has a family of eight planets orbiting around it, along with many **moons**, comets, and asteroids. Beyond the planets lie vast clouds of rock, metal, and ice.

Rocky planets

The planets closer to the Sun are also closer to each other. The Solar System began life as a cloud of dust and gas, and the Sun formed in its densest area. There was more rocky material to create planets in this area, so the rocky planets, also called the inner planets, formed closer together.

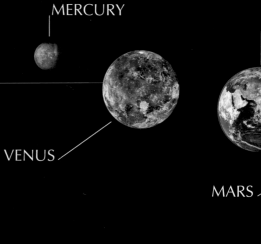

MERCURY

EARTH

VENUS

MARS

JUPITER

DISTANCES FROM THE SUN

Sun

Earth 93 million mi.
(150 million km)

Mars 142 million mi.
(228 million km)

Jupiter 484 million mi.
(778 million km)

Venus 67 million mi.
(108 million km)

Saturn
886 million mi.
(1427 million km)

Mercury 26 million mi.
(58 million km)

mass

A measure of the amount of matter contained in an object, such as a planet.

TOP FIVE **BITESIZE** FACTS

 Billions of years ago, there were dozens of planets in our Solar System.

 Our whole Solar System measures about 2 light-years across.

Venus is the hottest planet with a surface temperature of over 900 °F (400 °C).

The mass of Jupiter is 2.5 times more than the mass of all the other planets put together.

The Sun is almost 5 billion years old.

Building blocks

The inner planets are composed mainly of rock and metal. The outer planets are mostly ice and gas. This is because the Sun became so hot when it began to shine that only planets made of rock and metal could survive near it.

URANUS

NEPTUNE

SATURN

Uranus 1800 million mi.
(2871 million km)

Neptune
2800 million mi.
(4497 million km)

Light and heat

Our Sun is our Solar System's star. It is a vast ball of glowing gas so large that a million Earths would fit inside it. Without the Sun's light and heat, life on Earth would not be possible. Although the Sun is 90 million miles (150 million kilometers) away, its light is still bright enough to damage your eyes.

TOP FIVE BITESIZE FACTS

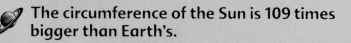

- The temperature of the Sun's surface is about 9900 °F (5500 °C).

- The temperature at the Sun's core is more than 18 million °F (15 million °C).

- The circumference of the Sun is 109 times bigger than Earth's.

- Every second, the Sun becomes 4 million tons lighter as it burns up its hydrogen.

- Without the Sun's heat, Earth's **atmosphere** would freeze.

Nuclear furnace

The Sun is made mostly of a substance called hydrogen. Inside the Sun's core, **nuclear reactions**, like those in atom bombs, convert the hydrogen into a gas called helium. This releases the enormous energy that we see as sunlight.

Sun sailing

The Sun's light gently presses against everything it touches. Solar sails are designed to be light, shiny craft that drift through space, pushed by sunlight just as sailing ships are pushed by wind. Solar sails may be used on future space probes or cargo ships.

A spacecraft powered by huge solar sails.

A prominence is a gigantic cloud of glowing gas that floats in the Sun's atmosphere.

Sunspots are dark patches on the Sun's surface. They are caused by the Sun's powerful **magnetic field**. They are darker than the rest of the Sun because they are cooler.

Solar eclipse

Every few months, the Moon passes directly between the Sun and Earth. When this happens, the Sun seems to turn black, and the glow of its corona appears around it. Normally, the Sun is too bright for the corona to be seen.

corona
The outer layer of a star's atmosphere.

Mercury and Venus

The planets Mercury and Venus are closer to the Sun than we are, so they are hotter than Earth. They also orbit the Sun more quickly.

Colorful craters

Like many photographs taken in space, this image by the **probe** *Mariner 10* has been falsely colored to show the different features more clearly.

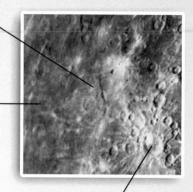

metal-rich area

solidified lava flow

Kuiper crater

No data have been recorded for this area, so it is left blank in images of the planet.

Mercury

Mercury is the smallest planet and the closest to the Sun. It cools rapidly at night because it has almost no atmosphere to trap the heat. The temperature can reach 800 °F (430 °C) by day, but nights are colder than in Antarctica. This image pieces together photographs taken by the *Mariner 10* probe. It discovered that the planet is rocky and cratered.

The surface of Mercury is marked with wrinkles. These probably formed when the planet cooled and shrank soon after it formed.

crater

A bowl-shaped area made by a fallen meteorite.

Mapping Venus

The thick clouds of Venus always hide its surface from our telescopes. In 1989, the *Magellan* probe was sent to orbit the planet and map its surface using **radar**. The probe showed that the surface of Venus is young—only half a billion years old.

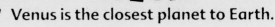
The *Magellan* probe orbited Venus for four years.

Only flashes of lightning brighten the cloudy, dark surface of Venus.

Maat Mons, the highest volcano on Venus

Venus

Venus was once thought to be similar to prehistoric Earth. In fact, Venus is a deadly planet with an atmosphere as dense as a liquid. Sulfuric acid rains down from the cloudy, yellow sky. The acid boils before reaching the ground. The thick atmosphere causes a **greenhouse effect** that heats the planet's surface to 900 °F (480 °C).

The 3-D maps of Venus produced by *Magellan* show that its rocky surface consists of mostly smooth, volcanic plains.

Planet Earth

The distance of Earth from the Sun is what makes life on our planet possible. Living things need liquid water. If we were much farther from the Sun, all our water would be frozen as it is on Mars. If we were a little closer, water would boil as it would on Venus.

The world is gradually heating up. As a result, the ice at the poles is melting. This causes flooding in low-lying areas.

Plants and trees produce oxygen, which all animals need to breathe. Plants also absorb the waste gases that animals breathe out.

TOP FIVE BITESIZE FACTS

- There has been life on Earth for more than three billion years.

- Night and day are caused by Earth spinning on its **axis**—one rotation takes 24 hours.

- If all the ice on Earth melted, the oceans and seas would rise by 330 feet (100 meters).

- Earth orbits the Sun at an average speed of 67,000 miles (108,000 kilometers) per hour.

- The oceans and seas cover around 75 percent of Earth's surface.

hemisphere
The northern or the southern half of Earth, which is divided in two by the line of the Equator.

People evolved only about 200,000 years ago, but they have transformed the planet. At night, the glow of city lights can be seen from space.

The seasons

Earth tilts on its axis. While one hemisphere is angled toward the Sun, the other is angled away from it. The hemisphere angled toward the Sun experiences summer while the other has winter. These seasons change as Earth completes its yearly orbit of the Sun.

Shifting plates

Earth's crust, a solid shell up to 30 miles (50 kilometers) thick, is broken up into vast pieces called plates. These plates are pushed around by the movement of hot, molten rock called magma below the surface. When plates collide or grind past each other, earthquakes occur and volcanoes erupt.

There are over seven million animal species on Earth. Each one is adapted to live in a particular place, like these penguins in their frozen Antarctic home.

Mars: the Red Planet

Mars, the Red Planet, is the second-closest planet to Earth and is the planet most like our own. It has ice caps, seasons, volcanoes, and deserts. In August 2012, the space agency NASA landed a rover called *Curiosity* on Mars to search for signs of life.

ExoMars rover

panoramic camera system to help the rover navigate an area of several square miles

solar panel

In 1976, the *Viking 2* probe landed on Mars and took this photograph. It shows a pink sky, caused by red dust particles in the atmosphere.

six rugged wheels to cope with the planet's rocky surface

ExoMars

The *ExoMars* rover (right) is due to begin its exploration of Mars in 2016. It is part of a European Space Agency (ESA) project. The rover will be delivered by a spacecraft that will remain in orbit, and will use balloons or parachutes to slow its descent for a safe landing. *ExoMars* uses **solar panels** for power and battery heaters to survive cold nights. Its mission is to search for past and present signs of life in the rocks and soil.

Ice on Mars

This bright-blue patch is a frozen pool of ice. It lies in a crater on the northern plains of Mars. The photograph was taken by ESA's *Mars Express Orbiter* in 2005. Although it was thought that water could not exist in liquid form on Mars because the atmospheric pressure is too low, liquid water was discovered in 2015.

TOP FIVE BITESIZE FACTS

 Mars is named after the Roman god of war.

The *Mars Reconnaissance Orbiter* reached the planet more than 10 years ago and is still sending back photos and other data.

Martian winds can create dust clouds more than 330 feet (100 meters) high.

Mars has two small moons called Deimos and Phobos.

Mars is red because it is rusty. Long ago, iron in the soil combined with oxygen to make the planet red.

atmospheric pressure
The weight of the air or other gases in a planet's atmosphere.

The frozen north

The *Reconnaissance Orbiter* took this photograph (right) of the northern polar region of Mars. It shows steep cliffs, about a mile (almost two kilometers) high, cloaked in ice.

Mars has permanently frozen ice at both its north and south poles. As on Earth, the ice caps grow or shrink according to the season.

Jupiter's Great Red Spot is a giant hurricane. It is much larger than Earth and has raged for centuries.

Ganymede is the largest moon in the Solar System.

Callisto is made largely of ice.

Io is sprinkled with erupting volcanoes.

Europa has liquid seas under its icy crust.

Jupiter and Saturn

Jupiter and Saturn are gas giants— huge worlds with deep, gassy atmospheres and cores of rock and ice. Both have rings around them. Jupiter's rings are faint dust belts, but Saturn's rings are made of rocky ice.

Many moons

Jupiter has at least 63 moons. The four shown above are the largest. They were first spotted in 1610 by the Italian astronomer Galileo Galilei (1564–1642). Other moons are captured asteroids just a few miles across.

Jupiter

Jupiter is the giant planet of the Solar System. Although it is more than four times as far from us as the Sun, its size can make it the brightest object in the night sky. The planet is surrounded by a zone of deadly **radiation** and an enormous magnetic field.

TOP FIVE BITESIZE FACTS

- Jupiter is large enough to contain all of the other planets in the Solar System.

- Saturn's atmosphere is 96 percent hydrogen.

- Jupiter's moon, Ganymede, is bigger than the planet Mercury.

- Because it spins so fast, Jupiter has a very short day. It lasts just 9 hours and 55 seconds.

- Jupiter and Saturn are still cooling after being formed. The heat causes storms that never end.

fragment
A piece broken off from something, such as rock.

Saturn's rings are shown in false color here. The pink rings contain only large rocks; the green and blue ones include smaller fragments as well.

Saturn

Saturn's rings are composed of billions of orbiting fragments of icy rock that range in size from tiny dust particles to large boulders. These fragments may be the remains of a moon-sized object that strayed too close to Saturn and was torn apart by the planet's gravity.

Uranus and Neptune

The two outermost planets of our Solar System are Uranus and Neptune. They are gas giants, like Jupiter and Saturn. Far out in space, the Sun shines dimly, so these planets are cold, dark worlds. They move slowly around the Sun on huge orbits. This gives them long years. One year on Uranus is 84 Earth-years and one year on Neptune is 165 Earth-years.

Miranda, a moon of Uranus

Uranus

Uranus was discovered in 1781 by English astronomer William Herschel (1738–1822). It was reached by a space probe 197 years later. Uranus is circled by rings of black boulders, and gets its green color from the methane gas in its atmosphere. The planet spins on its back, because it was knocked over by a collision with another planet billions of years ago.

TOP FIVE **BITESIZE** FACTS

 On some parts of Uranus, night can last for more than 40 Earth-years.

On Triton, the largest of Neptune's 13 moons, is covered in volcanoes that spew icy water and ammonia.

Uranus has 11 sparse rings.

Neptune has the most powerful winds ever known. They can reach speeds of more than 1200 miles (2160 kilometers) per hour.

There are 27 moons orbiting Uranus.

liquid nitrogen
The state of the gas nitrogen at an extremely low temperature.

Neptune

The blue color of the outermost planet in our Solar System comes from the methane in its atmosphere. The color also gives the planet its name as it was named after Neptune, the Roman god of the sea. This cold planet generates some heat of its own, which powers its dramatic weather systems. However, its largest moon, Triton, may be the coldest moon in the Solar System.

Vast, white clouds of frozen methane rush across a dark storm system on the face of Neptune, the windiest planet in the Solar System.

Nitrogen, which makes up most of our air, is mainly frozen solid on Neptune's moon, Triton.

Clouds of dust and gas

When people started to study the night sky with telescopes, they found fuzzy patches. They called these **nebulas**, which means clouds. Some nebulas are clouds of dust or gas. Others are nearby clusters of stars or distant galaxies.

The Eagle Nebula

These vast pillars of dust and gas form part of the Eagle Nebula. New stars are created here. Powerful radiation from nearby stars heats the outer layers of the columns to form a bluish green mist.

Star birth

This telescope image (left) shows the Eagle Nebula with an exploding star at its core. Exploding stars (supernovas) squeeze the surrounding cloud, forming dense, spinning discs of dust and gas. The center of the disc begins to glow with intense heat. Gravity keeps up the pressure until atoms fuse together and a star is born.

Small bulges contain globules of dense gas that are the beginnings of new stars.

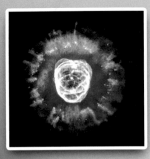

At only 1000 years old, the Eskimo Nebula is very young. Astronomer William Herschel discovered it in 1787.

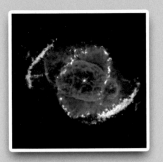

A planetary nebula is gas thrown off by a star. It is usually sphere-shaped but the Cat's Eye Nebula has a much more complex shape.

The Crab Nebula is the remains of a supernova—a massive star exploding at the end of its life. Light from the explosion was first spotted by Chinese astronomers in 1054.

TOP FIVE BITESIZE FACTS

- The Orion Nebula is the easiest to see from Earth.

- Nebulas are formed mainly from hydrogen and helium **molecules**.

- The first photograph of a nebula was taken by American scientist Henry Draper in 1870.

- Stars are created by nuclear reactions that produce light and heat.

- All the elements on Earth, including those in our own bodies, were once formed inside stars. We are literally made of star dust.

Each pillar is about one light-year long. This means that it would take light one year to travel from the top to the bottom.

The pillars may no longer exist, as a nearby supernova explosion might have destroyed them up to 6000 years ago. If so, we will not see that destruction for 1000 years as the pillars are 7000 light-years away.

globule
A small, dark nebula where stars begin to form.

How a star dies

Stars are like factories. They convert hydrogen to helium, and helium to other elements. This produces energy that lights our skies day and night. The nuclear processing goes on for billions of years until the hydrogen fuel finally runs out.

The nebula is made of thin gas and its core can be seen. The core is a **white dwarf**, which will take billions of years to cool.

When there is no fuel left to burn, the outer layers of a red giant swell, forming a planetary nebula.

When the hydrogen fuel in the core of a star runs out, nuclear reactions in its outer layers take over. This causes the star to swell and cool. It then turns into a **red giant**.

planetary nebula
A bubblelike nebula shaped like a planet.

Stars burn for millions or billions of years.

Two paths to death
Smallish stars like our Sun last for about 10 billion years. Stars with more mass have a shorter life—just a few million years. When a Sunlike star dies, its crushed core eventually becomes a remnant known as a white dwarf. Stars with greater mass, however, die in supernova explosions that are brighter than galaxies.

When they run out of hydrogen, massive stars swell up into supergiants. These may be a million times bigger than the Sun and a hundred thousand times brighter.

TOP FIVE BITESIZE FACTS

 VY Canis Majoris is the largest known star. It could hold about 10 billion Suns.

 The closest red giant to Earth is Gamma Crucis, 88 light-years away.

🪐 The hottest stars are called blue giants.

🪐 The first pulsar to be discovered was called LGM-1, short for Little Green Men, as some people thought the pulse was a signal from aliens.

🪐 Supernovas can both trigger the birth of new stars and provide the building materials for them.

Neutron stars form from the remains of supernovas. A pulsar is a type of neutron star. It has a magnetic field that sends out radio waves.

Inside a supergiant

Different nuclear reactions take place inside a supergiant. Elements are converted into other elements to release energy. When no further conversions are possible, the star collapses and then explodes as a supernova. This explosion scatters the different elements (shown here as different colors) through space.

Living in space

People are already living in space, in the International Space Station (ISS). This is the latest in a series of space stations. The first was the Soviet *Salyut 1* in 1971. The U.S.A. followed with the *Skylab* orbiting laboratory in 1973. Space stations are used for research, but in the far future, they may be used as hotels—and the first stepping stones for long-distance space explorers.

microgravity
The small gravitational pull felt inside spacecraft.

TOP FIVE BITESIZE FACTS

 The space station *Salyut 1* was only 65 feet (20 meters) long.

 The ISS is the size of a soccer pitch.

 Cosmonaut Valeriy Polyakov spent 437 days on the *Mir* space station in 1994–95—the longest single mission.

 As part of his training, British astronaut Tim Peake lived in a cave with no light and in an undersea station.

 In 2007, astronaut Sunita Williams ran a marathon in space on the ISS's treadmill.

Onboard the ISS

The ISS has been constructed in orbit by people from 16 countries. Onboard, the **astronauts** and other objects are almost weightless. The effects of this "microgravity" on people, plants, crystals, and fluids is being studied to help plan future space colonies. Without gravity, bones and muscles become weak, so astronauts must use exercise machines to stay strong.

Building a space station

The ISS has been assembled from separate modules, which were launched into space using rockets. The first module went into orbit in 1998 and the station has been permanently crewed since the first astronauts arrived in 2000. The station is powered by solar panels, which convert sunlight into electricity.

Living and working module

Robotic arm to dock spacecraft

Solar panels rotate to face the Sun.

Cooling plates radiate excess heat away from the station.

Soyuz space capsule returns crew to Earth in an emergency.

Astronauts construct the ISS 210 mi. (340km) above New Zealand.

Travel to the Stars

Traveling to the stars is now possible. Unmanned probes are now heading for the farthest reaches of the Solar System. Crossing vast distances is not the problem, but the probes will travel for tens of thousands of years before reaching a star. For people to explore other star systems, faster ships are needed.

TOP FIVE BITESIZE FACTS

 Astronauts in *Apollo 10* traveled farthest from Earth—248,655 miles (400,171 kilometers).

 The nearest star is about one million times farther from Earth than the nearest planet.

 If it could achieve one third of light-speed, an interstellar ramjet would still take 13 years to reach the nearest star.

 NASA's *Voyager 1* and *Voyager 2* probes have been traveling through space for 39 years.

Saturn *Voyager 1* is now over 12 billion miles (20 billion kilometers) away from Earth.

Landing craft

Spaceships will not be designed to land on other worlds. Instead, crews will descend to planets in short-range shuttle craft that have streamlined shapes for flying through planetary atmospheres.

interstellar
Between the stars.

Interstellar ramjet

All spaceships need fuel and material called reaction mass. This is blasted away from them, to provide thrust in the opposite direction. To avoid carrying too much weight, an interstellar ramjet would draw gas from space. Gas will fuel its reactors and act as reaction mass.

A metal web generates an **electromagnetic** field to "scoop up" interstellar gas (mostly hydrogen).

Voyages may last for centuries, so astronauts will be deep-cooled inside **hibernation** pods, allowing them to sleep for decades.

An **antenna** enables communication with Earth.

crew area

A shield protects crew areas from the radiation of the reactors.

fuel tanks

Two types of hydrogen (deuterium and tritium) undergo nuclear fusion. This produces neutrons, helium and energy to power the ramjet.

exhaust gases, including helium

Glossary

antenna
A metal structure used to transmit or receive radio signals. Antenna is another name for an aerial.

astronaut
A person, often a scientist, who is trained to travel into space.

atmosphere
A layer of gas that surrounds a planet, a star, or a moon.

atom
The tiniest object from which everything is made. Atoms combine to make molecules.

axis
An imaginary line running through a planet from the north to the south pole.

cosmonaut
An astronaut trained by Russia.

electromagnetic
Describes the electric and magnetic energy around particles.

element
A substance such as hydrogen or helium that contains only one type of atom.

galaxy
A collection of millions, billions, or even trillions of stars, which are held together by gravity.

gravity
A natural force that draws all objects toward one another. The strength of the force depends on the mass of the objects.

greenhouse effect
The way that a planet's atmosphere can trap heat from the Sun, making the planet hotter.

hibernation
A deep sleep where the body's functions slow to a rate that maintains life for a long period.

magnetic field
The area of magnetic energy projected by a body that may be as small as a particle or as large as a planet.

matter
A substance made up of atoms or the particles that combine to make atoms.

molecule
Two or more atoms held together by chemical bonds.

moon
A solid body that orbits a planet. Also known as a natural satellite.

nebula

A gas or dust cloud in space where new stars are formed.

neutron star

A dead, former massive star in which gravity is extremely high. A neutron star is the remnant of a supernova explosion.

nuclear reaction

In stars, a process in which the nuclei of hydrogen atoms merge to form other elements and release energy.

orbit

The path of one object around another in space, such as a planet around a star.

particle

An extremely small piece of matter.

planet

A body of rock, metal, or gas that is smaller than a star and is held in orbit around a star.

probe

An unmanned spacecraft on a mission to explore other worlds and gather information.

radar

Short for RAdio Detection And Ranging, radar uses radio waves to detect and to locate distant objects.

radiation

Energy, such as heat, light, or radio waves, that spreads outward, or radiates, through space from its source.

red giant

A dying stage of a Sunlike star, which forms when the star runs out of hydrogen and begins to burn helium.

solar panel

A device that converts the light from the Sun into electricity.

white dwarf

A dead, former Sunlike star. A white dwarf may be no larger than Earth, but can have a mass similar to that of the Sun.

Universe

Everything in existence, including all matter and all space. Scientists calculate that the Universe is 13.7 billion years old.

Index

A

Akatsuki probe 13
Andromeda Galaxy 6
antenna 29, 30
antimatter 4, 30
Apollo 10 28
asteroids 8, 18
astronauts 26, 27, 28, 29
atmospheres 10–13, 16–21, 28, 30
atoms 5, 22, 30, 31

B, C

Big Bang 4, 5
Big Chill theory 5
Big Rip theory 5
blue giant stars 25
Callisto 18
comets 8
cosmonauts 26
craters 12, 17
Curiosity rover 16

D, E

dark energy 4
dark matter 4
Eagle Nebula 22, 23
Earth 7, 8, 9, 10, 11, 12, 13, 14, 15, 17, 18, 23, 25, 27, 28, 29
electromagnetic fields 29, 30
elements 5, 23, 24, 25, 30, 31
energy 4, 10, 24, 25, 29, 30, 31
Europa 18
European Space Agency 16
ExoMars rover 16

G

galaxies 5, 6, 7, 22, 24
Galilei, Galileo 18
Ganymede 18, 19
gravity 4, 7, 19, 22, 26, 30, 31
greenhouse effect 13, 30

H, I, J

helium 5, 10, 23, 24, 29, 30, 31
Herschel, William 20, 23
hydrogen 5, 10, 19, 23, 24, 29, 30, 31
ice 9, 14, 16, 17, 18
International Space Station 26–27
Io 18
Jupiter 8, 9, 18, 19, 20

M, N

Maat Mons 13
Magellan probe 13
magnetic fields 11, 19, 25, 30
Mariner 10 12–13
Mars 8, 14, 16, 17
Mars Express Orbiter 17
Mars Reconnaissance Orbiter 17
Mercury 8, 12, 13
meteorite 12
Milky Way 6, 7
Miranda 20
moons 8, 17, 18, 20, 21, 30, 31
NASA 16, 28
nebulas 22, 23, 24, 31
Neptune 9, 20–21
neutron stars 25, 31
neutrons 29
nuclear reactions 10, 23, 24, 25, 29, 31

O, P

Orion Nebula 23
oxygen 14, 17
probes 11, 12, 13, 16, 20, 28
pulsars 25

R, S

radar 13, 31
radiation 19, 22, 29, 31
radio waves 25, 31
ramjet 28–29
red giant stars 24, 25, 31
Saturn 8, 9, 18–19, 20
seasons 15, 16
solar eclipse 11
solar panels 16, 27, 31
solar prominences 11
solar sails 11
Solar System 7, 8–9, 18, 19, 20, 21, 28
space stations 26–27
spaceships 11, 28–29
stars 4, 5, 6, 7, 11, 22, 23, 24–25, 28, 30, 31
Sun 4, 5, 10, 11, 12, 13, 14, 15, 19, 20, 24, 25, 27, 30, 31
sunspots 11
supergiant stars 24, 25
supernovas 5, 22, 23, 24, 25, 31

T, U

telescopes 13, 22
Triton 21
Universe 4, 5, 6, 7
Uranus 9, 20, 21

V, W

Venus 8, 12, 13, 14
Viking 2 16
volcanoes 13, 15, 16, 18, 21
Voyager probes 28
Whirlpool Galaxy 7
white dwarf stars 24, 31